THUNDERING SILENCE

Other Books by Thich Nhat Hanh

Be Free Where You Are

Being Peace

Breathe! You Are Alive: Sutra on the Full Awareness of Breathing

Call Me by My True Names: The Collected Poems of Thich Nhat Hanh

Cultivating the Mind of Love: The Practice of Looking Deeply in the Mahayana Buddhist Tradition

The Diamond That Cuts through Illusion: Commentaries on the Prajñaparamita Diamond Sutra

Finding our True Home: Living in the Pure Land Here and Now

For a Future to Be Possible: Commentaries on the Five Mindfulness Trainings

Fragrant Palm Leaves: Journals 1962-1966

Friends on the Path: Living Spiritual Communities

The Heart of the Buddha's Teaching: Transforming Suffering into Peace, Joy, and Liberation

The Heart of Understanding: Commentaries on the Prajñaparamita Heart Sutra

I Have Arrived, I Am Home

Interbeing: Fourteen Guidelines for Engaged Buddhism

Joyfully Together: The Art of Building a Harmonious Community

The Long Road Turns to Joy: A Guide to Walking Meditation

Love in Action: Writings on Nonviolent Social Change

Master Tang Hoi: First Zen Teacher in Vietnam & China

My Master's Robe: Memories of a Novice Monk

Old Path White Clouds: Walking in the Footsteps of the Buddha

Opening the Heart of the Cosmos: Insights on the Lotus Sutra

Our Appointment with Life: Discourse on Living Happily in the Present Moment

The Path of Emancipation

Plum Village Chanting and Recitation Book

Present Moment Wonderful Moment: Mindfulness Verses for Daily Living

A Rose for Your Pocket

Stepping into Freedom: An Introduction to Buddhist Monastic Training

The Stone Boy and Other Stories

The Sun My Heart: From Mindfulness to Insight Contemplation

Sutra on the Eight Realizations of the Great Beings

A Taste of Earth and Other Legends of Vietnam

Teachings on Love

Thundering Silence: Sutra on Knowing the Better Way to Catch a Snake

Touching Peace: Practicing the Art of Mindful Living

Transformation and Healing: Sutra on the Four Establishments of Mindfulness

Transformation at the Base: Fifty Verses on the Nature of Consciousness

THUNDERING SILENCE

Sutra on Knowing
the Better Way to Catch a Snake

THICH NHAT HANH

Translated from the Vietnamese
by Annabel Laity

Parallax Press
Berkeley, California

Parallax Press
P.O. Box 7355
Berkeley, CA 94707
www.parallax.org

Parallax Press is the publishing division of Unified Buddhist Church, Inc.

Cover art by Hieu De.
Cover design by Gay Reineck.
Text design by Ayelet Maida.

Library of Congress Cataloging-in-Publication Data
Tipitaka. Suttapitaka. Majjhimanikaya. Alagaddupama Sutta.
English
Thundering silence: sutra on knowing the better way to
catch a snake / Thich Nhat Hanh; translated from the
Vietnamese by Annabel Laity.
p. cm.
ISBN 0-938077-64-3 (paper)
I. Nhât Hanh, Thích. II. Laity, Annabel. III. Title.
BQ1320.A4222E5 1993
294.3'823—dc20   93-31387
                                                     CIP

8 9 10 11 12 13 / 08 07 06 05 04 03

Contents

Introduction

I studied the *Diamond Sutra* for more than twenty years before I had the opportunity to encounter the *Sutra on Knowing the Better Way to Catch a Snake.* I was very happy to discover it because I realized that the simile of the raft and the "thundering silence" statement made by the Buddha — "You have to let go even of the true Dharma, not to mention the non-Dharma" — in the *Diamond Sutra* have their roots in the *Sutra on Knowing the Better Way to Catch a Snake.*

The snake simile is also very special. The Buddha urges us to study and practice the Dharma in an intelligent way so we will not be caught by notions and words, like a person who knows how to catch a snake without being bitten. I had never before heard anyone compare his or her teaching to a snake or say that it can be dangerous to learn and practice, and I was impressed.

Although his teachings are deep, the Buddha likes to present them in a simple way. While describing the interdependent-origination nature of reality, for instance, he simply says, "This is, because that is." This may not sound difficult, but it is very profound, and many have misunderstood it, including people of his own time, even some monks and nuns who had the opportunity to hear the Buddha directly. It is no wonder that scholars and practitioners of later generations have misunderstood and misrepresented his teachings. Many people think, for example, that the Buddha teaches of nonbeing, annihilation, the destruction of all feelings and intentions, the dissolution of individualities into nirvana, and so forth. The teachings of emptiness, nonself, nirvana, non-obtaining, *tathagata,* etc., continue to be misunderstood, from generation to generation.

In the *Sutra on Knowing the Better Way to Catch a Snake,* the Buddha reminds us to be skillful and careful in learning and practicing, and not to be caught by words or notions. The teachings of emptiness, nonself, nirvana, etc., are cited in the sutra as examples of misrepresentations. The sutra affords us another opportunity to receive the teaching.

"During forty-five years, I have not said anything." This statement by the Buddha warns us not to be caught by words or notions. It is truly the roar of a great lion. If we get caught by words or notions, we will not be able to receive the true teachings of the Buddha. For this reason, we have given this book the title, *Thundering Silence.* May the *Sutra on Knowing the Better Way to Catch a Snake* sweep away the fog of words and notions in us so that the sun of the true teaching can shine brightly on the field of our understanding mind.

SUTRA ON KNOWING
THE BETTER WAY
TO CATCH A SNAKE

Sutra on Knowing
the Better Way to Catch a Snake

I heard these words one time when the Buddha was staying at the Anathapindika Monastery in the Jeta Park, near Shravasti. At that time, the Bhikshu Arittha, who before being ordained had been a vulture trainer,[1] had the wrong view that according to the teachings of the Buddha, sense pleasures are not an obstacle to the practice. After hearing this, many bhikshus went to Arittha and asked, "Brother Arittha, do you really believe that the Buddha teaches that sense pleasures are not an obstacle to the practice?"

Arittha replied, "Yes, friends, it is true that I believe the Buddha does not regard sense pleasures as an obstacle to the practice."

The bhikshus scolded him, "Brother Arittha, you misrepresent the Buddha's teachings and even slander him. The Lord has never said that sense pleasures are not an obstacle to the practice. In fact, he uses many examples to teach that sense pleasures *are* an obstacle to the practice. You should abandon your wrong view." Although the bhikshus counseled Arittha in this way, he was not moved to change his view. Three times they asked him to abandon his wrong view, and three times he refused, continuing to say that he was right and the others were wrong.

So the bhikshus went to the hut of the Buddha, prostrated at the Lord's feet, sat to one side, and addressed him respect-

---

[1] Arittha is referred to here as a "vulture trainer" to distinguish him from other monks with the same name.

fully, "World-Honored One, the Bhikshu Arittha says that according to the teachings of the Lord, sense pleasures are not an obstacle to the practice. We asked him three times to abandon his wrong view, but he continues to hold to this view. So we have come to you, Lord. What should we do?"

Hearing this, the Buddha asked one of the bhikshus to invite Arittha to come to his hut. The bhikshu stood up, prostrated himself, circumambulated the Buddha three times, and went to Bhikshu Arittha. When Arittha heard that the Lord wanted to see him, he came right away, prostrated before the Buddha, and sat to one side. The Buddha said, "Arittha, is it true you have been saying that I teach that sense pleasures are not an obstacle to the practice?"

Arittha replied, "Yes, Lord — I do believe that according to the spirit of your teachings, sense pleasures are not an obstacle to the practice."

The Lord admonished him. "Arittha, what could have led you to that view? When did you ever hear me teach that sense pleasures are not an obstacle to the practice? Who has said that I teach that? Arittha, you are not correct. Your brothers in the Dharma have advised you to drop your wrong view, and you should." The Buddha then asked the other monks, "Bhikshus, have you ever heard me teach that sense pleasures are not an obstacle to the practice?"

The bhikshus replied, "No, Lord, we have not."

The Buddha then asked, "What have you heard me teach?"

The bhikshus replied, "We have heard the Lord teach that sense pleasures are an obstacle to the practice. Lord, you have said that sense pleasures are like a skeleton, a piece of raw meat, a straw torch, a pit of burning charcoal, a poisonous snake, a dream, borrowed belongings, or a tree laden with fruit."[2]

The Lord said, "Bhikshus, that is correct. I have always taught that sense pleasures are an obstacle to the practice. Sense pleasures are like a skeleton, a piece of raw meat, a straw torch, a pit of burning charcoal, a poisonous snake, a dream, borrowed belongings, or a tree laden with fruit. Bhikshu Arittha, you have misunderstood both the letter and the spirit of my teachings. You have presented my teachings as the opposite of what I intended. You have misrepresented and even slandered me, and, at the same time, you have done harm to yourself and others. This is a serious transgression that will cause noble teachers and sincere practitioners much sadness." Hearing the Lord's reprimand, Bhikshu Arittha bowed his head in silence. He was hurt and upset, and could think of nothing at all to say.

After admonishing Arittha this way, the Buddha taught all of the bhikshus, "Monks, it is important to understand my teachings thoroughly before you teach or put them into practice. If you have not understood the meaning of any teaching I give, please ask me or one of the elder brothers in the Dharma or one of the others who is excellent in the practice about it. There are always some people who do not understand the letter or the spirit of a teaching and, in fact, take it the opposite way of what was intended, whether the teachings are offered in the form of verse or prose, predictions, verse summaries, interdependent origination, similes, spontaneous utterances, quotations, stories of previous births, wonderful occurrences, detailed commentaries,

---

[2] The Pali version adds two other comparisons: an impaling stake and a slaughterhouse.

or clarifications with definitions.[3] There are always some people who study only to satisfy their curiosity or win arguments, and not for the sake of liberation. With such a motivation, they miss the true spirit of the teaching. They may go through much hardship, endure difficulties that are not of much benefit, and eventually exhaust themselves.

"Bhikshus, a person who studies that way can be compared to a man trying to catch a poisonous snake in the wild. If he reaches out his hand, the snake may bite his hand, leg, or some other part of his body. Trying to catch a snake that way has no advantages and can only create suffering.

"Bhikshus, understanding my teaching in the wrong way is the same. If you do not practice the Dharma correctly, you may come to understand it as the opposite of what was intended. But if you practice intelligently, you will understand both the letter and the spirit of the teachings and will be able to explain them correctly. Do not practice just to show off or argue with others. Practice to attain liberation, and if you do, you will have little pain or exhaustion.

"Bhikshus, an intelligent student of the Dharma is like a man who uses a forked stick to catch a snake. When he sees a poisonous snake in the wild, he places the stick right below the head of the snake and grabs the snake's neck with his hand. Even if the snake winds itself around the man's hand, leg, or another part of his body, it will not bite him. This is

---

[3] In the Pali version there are only nine divisions of the teachings. The Chinese version gives all twelve: 1. Discourses *(sutra)* 2. Teachings in verse *(geya)* 3. Predictions *(vyakarana)* 4. Summaries in verse *(gatha)* 5. Interdependent origination *(nidana)* 6. Instructions by simile *(upadesha)* 7. Quotations *(itivrittaka)* 8. Inspired sayings *(udana)* 9. Stories of previous births *(jataka)* 10. Extensive explanations *(vaipulya)* 11. Wonderful teachings *(adbhuta dharma)* 12. Giving definitions *(avadana)*.

the better way to catch a snake, and it will not lead to pain or exhaustion.

"Bhikshus, a son or daughter of good family who studies the Dharma needs to apply the utmost skill to understanding the letter and the spirit of the teachings. He or she should not study with the aim of boasting, debating, or arguing, but only to attain liberation. Studying in this way, with intelligence, he or she will have little pain or exhaustion.

"Bhikshus, I have told you many times the importance of knowing when it is time to let go of a raft and not hold onto it unnecessarily. When a mountain stream overflows and becomes a torrent of floodwater carrying debris, a man or woman who wants to get across might think, 'What is the safest way to cross this floodwater?' Assessing the situation, she may decide to gather branches and grasses, construct a raft, and use it to cross to the other side. But, after arriving on the other side, she thinks, 'I spent a lot of time and energy building this raft. It is a prized possession, and I will carry it with me as I continue my journey.' If she puts it on her shoulders or head and carries it with her on land, bhikshus, do you think that would be intelligent?"

The bhikshus replied, "No, World-Honored One."

The Buddha said, "How could she have acted more wisely? She could have thought, 'This raft helped me get across the water safely. Now I will leave it at the water's edge for someone else to use in the same way.' Wouldn't that be a more intelligent thing to do?"

The bhikshus replied, "Yes, World-Honored One."

The Buddha taught, "I have given this teaching on the raft many times to remind you how necessary it is to let go of all the true teachings, not to mention teachings that are not true."

~

"Bhikshus, there are six bases for views.[4] This means that there are six grounds of wrong perception that we need to drop. What are the six?

"First, there is body. Whether belonging to the past, the future, or the present, whether it is our own body or the body of someone else, whether subtle or gross, ugly or beautiful, near or far, the body is not mine, is not me, is not the self. Bhikshus, please look deeply so that you can see the truth concerning the body.

"Second, there are feelings.

"Third, there are perceptions.

"(Fourth, there are mental formations.)[5] Whether these phenomena belong to the past, the future, or the present, whether they are our own or someone else's, whether they are subtle or gross, ugly or beautiful, near or far, such phenomena are not mine, are not me, are not the self.

"Fifth, there is consciousness. Whatever we see, hear, perceive, know, mentally grasp, observe, or think about at the present time or any other time is not ours, is not us, is not the self.

"Sixth, there is the world. Some people think, 'The world is the self. The self is the world. The world is me. I will continue to exist without changing even after I die. I am eternal.

---

[4] "Grounds for views" are the foundations that cause us to cling to views (Sanskrit: *drshtisthana;* Pali: *ditthithana*).

[5] The Chinese version is missing the fourth *skandha*, mental formations (Sanskrit: *samskara;* Pali: *sankhara*).

I will never disappear.' Please meditate so you can see that the world is not mine, is not me, is not the self. Please look deeply so you can see the truth concerning the world."[6]

~

Upon hearing this, one bhikshu stood up, bared his right shoulder, joined his palms respectfully, and asked the Buddha, "World-Honored One, can fear and anxiety arise from an internal source?"[7]

The Buddha replied, "Yes, fear and anxiety can arise from an internal source. If you think, 'Things that did not exist in the past have come to exist, but now no longer exist,' you will feel sad or become confused and despairing. This is how fear and anxiety can arise from an internal source."

The same bhikshu then asked, "World-Honored One, can fear and anxiety from an internal source be prevented from arising?"

The Buddha replied, "Fear and anxiety from an internal source can be prevented from arising. If you do not think, 'Things that did not exist in the past have come to exist, but now no longer exist,' you will not feel sad or become confused and despairing. This is how fear and anxiety from an internal source can be prevented from arising."

"World-Honored One, can fear and anxiety arise from an external source?"

The Buddha taught, "Fear and anxiety can arise from an external source. You may think, 'This is a self. This is the

---

[6] This sentence is not found in the Pali version. Instead, we find the following sentence: "When he understands that the self does not exist in this way, he is not upset."

[7] The Pali version speaks of an external source first and an internal source second.

world. This is myself. I will exist forever.' Then if you meet the Buddha or a disciple of the Buddha who has the understanding and intelligence to teach you how to let go of all views of attachment to the body, the self, and the objects of the self with a view to giving up pride, internal formations,[8] and energy leaks,[9] and you think, 'This is the end of the world. I have to give up everything. I am not the world. I am not me. I am not the self. I will not exist forever. When I die, I will be completely annihilated. There is nothing to look forward to, to be joyful about, or to remember,' you will feel sad and become confused and despairing. This is how fear and anxiety can arise from an external source."

"World-Honored One, can fear and anxiety from an external source be prevented from arising?"

The Buddha taught, "Fear and anxiety from an external source can be prevented from arising if you do not think, 'This is the self. This is the world. This is myself. I will exist forever.' Then if you meet the Buddha or a disciple of the Buddha who has the understanding and intelligence to teach you how to let go of all views of attachment to the body, the self, and the objects of the self with a view to giving up pride, internal formations, and energy leaks, and you do not think, 'This is the end of the world. I have to give up everything. I am not the world. I am not me. I am not the self. I will not exist forever. When I die I will be completely annihilated.

---

[8] Internal formations are the psychological ropes that bind us, like knots of afflictions stored in the depths of our consciousness (Sanskrit and Pali: *samyojana*).

[9] Energy leaks are the afflictions that lengthen the time we suffer and tie us to the realm of birth and death. *Ashrava* is the Sanskrit word; the Pali is *asava;* and the literal meaning is "to leak." The meaning can also be that of "affliction," synonymous with the Sanskrit *klesha* and Pali *kilesa*.

There is nothing to look forward to, to be joyful about, or to remember,' you will not feel sad or become confused and despairing. This is how fear and anxiety from an external source can be prevented from arising."

Hearing these words, the bhikshu praised and thanked the Buddha, completely accepted the Lord's teaching, and then kept silent.

~

The Buddha asked, "Bhikshus, do you think the Five Aggregates and the self are permanent, changeless, and not subject to destruction?"

"No, reverend teacher."

"Is there anything you can hold onto with attachment that will not cause anxiety, exhaustion, sorrow, suffering, and despair?"

"No, reverend teacher."

"Is there any view of self in which you can take refuge that will not cause anxiety, exhaustion, sorrow, suffering, and despair?"

"No, reverend teacher."

"Bhikshus, you are quite correct. Whenever there is an idea of self, there is also an idea of what belongs to the self. When there is no idea of self, there is no idea of anything that belongs to the self. Self and what belongs to the self are two views that are based on trying to grasp things that cannot be grasped and to establish things that cannot be established.[10] Such wrong perceptions cause us to be bound by

---

[10] "Cannot be grasped" is translated from the Chinese *bu ke de, bu ke shi she* (Sanskrit: *anupalabhya,* "not to be grasped").

internal formations that arise the moment we are caught by ideas that cannot be grasped or established and have no basis in reality. Do you see that these are wrong perceptions? Do you see the consequences of such wrong perceptions in the case of Bhikshu Arittha?"

The bhikshus replied, "Yes, reverend teacher. These are wrong perceptions, and the consequences of such wrong perceptions can be seen in the case of Bhikshu Arittha."

∿

The Buddha continued, "If, when he considers the six bases for wrong views,[11] a bhikshu does not give rise to the idea of 'I' or 'mine,' he is not caught in the chains of this life. Since he is not caught in the chains of this life, he has no fear. To have no fear is to arrive at nirvana. Such a person is no longer troubled by birth and death; the holy life has been lived; what needs to be done has been done; there will be no further births or deaths; and the truth of things as they are is known. Such a bhikshu has filled in the moat, crossed the moat, destroyed the enemy citadel, unbolted the door, and is able to look directly into the mirror of highest understanding.

"What is meant by 'filling in the moat'? 'Filling in the moat' means to know and clearly understand the substance of ignorance. Ignorance has been uprooted and shattered and cannot arise anymore.

"What is meant by 'crossing the moat'? 'Crossing the moat' means to know and clearly understand the substance

---

[11] See page 8.

of becoming and craving.[12] Becoming and craving have been uprooted and shattered and cannot arise anymore.

"What is meant by 'destroying the enemy citadel'? 'Destroying the enemy citadel' means to know and clearly understand the substance of the cycle of birth and death. The cycle of birth and death has been uprooted and shattered and cannot arise anymore.

"What is meant by 'unbolting the door'? 'Unbolting the door' means to know and clearly understand the substance of the five dull internal formations.[13] The five dull internal formations have been uprooted and shattered and cannot arise anymore.

"What is meant by 'looking directly into the mirror of highest understanding'? 'Looking directly into the mirror of highest understanding' means to know and understand clearly the substance of pride. Pride has been uprooted and shattered and cannot arise anymore.

"Bhikshus, that is the Way of the Tathagata and those who have attained liberation. Indra, Prajapati,[14] Brahma, and the other gods in their entourage, however hard they look, cannot find any trace or basis for the consciousness of a

---

[12] "Becoming" (Sanskrit: *bhava*) refers to being born and dying in a cycle of birth and death. "Craving" (Sanskrit: *trishna*) and "becoming" are two of the twelve links of interdependent origination (Sanskrit: *dvadashanga pratitya samutpada*).

[13] The first five internal formations are desire, hatred, ignorance, pride, and doubt. They are sometimes called "dull." The other five internal knots are personality views, extreme views, wrong views, perverted views, and views relating to rituals and prohibitions, and are sometimes called "sharp."

[14] According to Indian mythology, Prajapati (Pali: *Pajapati*) is the progenitor or the creator of the world. This role is sometimes given to Indra, Savitri, Soma, Manu, and other deities.

Tathagata.[15] The Tathagata is a noble fount of freshness and coolness. There is no great heat and no sorrow in this state. When recluses and brahmans hear me say this, they may slander me, saying that I do not speak the truth, that the monk Gautama proposes a theory of nihilism and teaches absolute nonexistence, while in fact living beings do exist. Bhikshus, the Tathagata has never taught the things they say. In truth, the Tathagata teaches only the ending of suffering in order to attain the state of non-fear. If the Tathagata is blamed, criticized, defamed, or defeated, he does not care. He does not become angry, walk away in hatred, or do anything in revenge. If someone blames, criticizes, defames, or defeats the Tathagata, how does he react? The Tathagata thinks, 'If someone respects, honors, or makes offerings to a Tathagata, the Tathagata would not on that account feel pleased. He would think only that someone is doing this because the Tathagata has attained the fruits of awakening and transformation.'

"Bhikshus, if people blame, criticize, defame, or defeat you, or respect, honor, or make offerings to you, there is no need on either account to feel angry or pleased, nor to do anything in revenge. Why? If you look deeply, you will see that there is no 'I' and no 'mine.' If someone were to walk around the grounds of this monastery and pick up the dead branches and dried grass to take home and burn or use in some other way, should we think that it is we ourselves who are being taken home to be burned or used in some way?"

---

[15] The Chinese version lacks the following sentence that appears in the Pali version: "I say that right here and now it is impossible to find any trace of the Tathagata." This sentence is also found in the *Anuradha Sutta* (*Samyutta Nikaya*, Vol. III, p. 118).

"No, reverend teacher."

"It is the same when someone praises, honors, or makes offerings to us, or blames, criticizes, or defames us. We should not rejoice or become angry. Why? It is because there are no such things as 'I' or 'mine.'

"The true teachings have been illuminated and made available in the worlds of humans and gods, with nothing lacking. If someone with right understanding penetrates these teachings, the value will be immeasurable. If, at the time of passing from this life, someone has been able to transform the five dull internal formations, in the next life he or she will attain nirvana. That person will arrive at the state of non-returner and will not reenter the cycle of birth and death. If, at the time of passing from this life, someone has been able to transform the three internal formations of attachment, aversion, and ignorance, he or she will be born only one more time in the worlds of humans or gods in order to be liberated. If, at the time of passing from this life, someone has been able to attain the fruit of stream-enterer, he or she will not fall again into states of extreme suffering and will surely go in the direction of right awakening. After being born seven times in the worlds of humans or gods, he or she will come to the place of liberation. If, at the time of passing from this life, someone has faith in understanding the teachings, he or she will be born in a blessed world and will continue to progress on the path to highest awakening."

Having heard the Buddha speak thus, the bhikshus, with great joy, put the teachings into practice.

COMMENTARIES

Commentaries

1
THE PURPOSE OF THIS SUTRA

When we study the Buddha's teachings, we have to be careful to understand them correctly. If we misunderstand the teachings of the Buddha, it is not only unfair to the Buddha, it can also be harmful to ourselves and others. We should not study the Dharma just to become a skilled debater or to show off the knowledge that we have accumulated. The only reason to study the Dharma is to put it into practice. The teachings on no-self and nirvana are deep and wonderful, but they are very easy to misunderstand. We must study them in a serious and sincere way. Many of the Buddha's contemporaries, even some of his own disciples, misunderstood him, so, of course, we also might misunderstand. The teachings of the Buddha are not a philosophy. They are a path, a raft to help us get across the river of suffering.

In the *Sutra on Knowing the Better Way to Catch a Snake,* the Buddha tells us to use great care and skill while studying and practicing his teachings. He uses two wonderful examples, catching a snake properly and giving up your raft after you have crossed the river, that have made this sutra very well-known.

2
CIRCUMSTANCES UNDER WHICH
THE SUTRA WAS DELIVERED

The Buddha spoke these words when one of his disciples, Arittha, had been telling his fellow monks that he understood the Buddha's teachings to say that sense pleasures are not an obstacle to the practice. After telling Arittha that he had misunderstood his teachings, the Buddha taught Arittha and the other bhikshus the *Sutra on Knowing the Better Way to Catch a Snake.*

3
THE TITLE

In the Southern tradition, this sutra is recorded in Pali in the *Alagaddupama Sutta,* which means "Snake Simile." It is in the *Majjhima Nikaya,* Sutta No. 22. In the Northern tradition, the same sutra is recorded in Chinese as the *Arittha Sutra.* The Chinese version is in the *Madhyama Agama,* Sutra No. 220. In the *Taisho Revised Tripitaka,* the *Madhyama Agama* is No. 26. This sutra was translated by Gautama Sanghadeva from Sanskrit into Chinese in the years 397–398.

4
ARITTHA'S MISUNDERSTANDING

Bhikshu Arittha had been saying that according to the teaching of the Buddha, sense pleasures are not an obstacle to the practice. Why was it that even though all the other bhikshus understood that sense pleasures bring suffering and the bonds of attachment, Bhikshu Arittha continued to say that sense pleasures are not an obstacle to the practice? Should we surmise that Arittha lacked intelligence to such an extent that he was incapable of understanding this simple and basic teaching? Or should we think that he wanted to distort the teaching or advocate the opposite of what the Buddha taught?

Who was Bhikshu Arittha? We are told that before becoming a monk, he had been a vulture trainer. In the *Arittha Sutta* that is found in the *Samyutta Nikaya* (Vol. v, pp. 314–315), the Buddha asks some monks whether they practice mindfulness of breathing. Arittha says that he does, and he explains to the Buddha the way he practices. The Buddha does not comment on what he says but goes on to teach the bhikshus several practices to further increase their concentration.

In the *Vinaya Pitaka* of the Southern tradition, we read how Bhikshu Arittha, after being asked by other bhikshus three times to refrain from speaking the wrong view presented in this sutra, was accused of a *pacittaya* offense by the Sangha in Chabbaggiya, a place not far from Shravasti, and we are told that he received the penalty of *ukkhepaniya kamma,* suspension from the order (*Vinaya* Vol. ii, p. 25–8). We see that during the time of his suspension, a number of bhikshus and a bhikshuni, Thullananda (*Vinaya* Vol. iv, p. 218), stayed in contact with him and, as a result, were also suspended (*Vinaya* Vol. iv, p. 137). In reading the *Sutra on Knowing the Better Way to Catch a Snake,* I have the feeling that although Bhikshu Arittha was willful, he was not unintelligent. From other sources, we see that his views as well as his personality were able to influence other bhikshus and bhikshunis. So we need to examine how it was that he misunderstood this teaching of the Buddha and continued to hold to his view.

In my opinion, Arittha's misunderstanding stems from his failure to see the difference between attachment to sense pleasures and the joy and happiness that arise from a peaceful mind. On many occasions, the Buddha taught that joy and happiness are nourishing to us, while indulging in sense pleasures can cause us suffering. What is the difference? Let us first discuss what is meant by the joy and happiness of a mindful and peaceful person.

Many people think that to undergo spiritual discipline is to practice asceticism and austerities. But to others, the practice of the Dharma does not exclude the enjoyment of the fresh air, the setting sun, a glass of cool water, and so on. Enjoying things in moderation does not bring us suffering or tie us with the bonds of attachment. Once we recognize that all of these things are impermanent, we have no problem enjoying them. In fact, real peace and joy are only possible when we see clearly into the nature of impermanence.

The Buddha often revealed himself as someone who was able to appreciate these kinds of simple joys. When Mahanama, the King of Kapilavastu, offered the Sangha a delicious lunch, the Buddha knew it was a good meal and expressed appreciation for it. When he was standing with Ananda on a hill overlooking an expanse of golden rice fields, the Buddha told Ananda how beautiful he found the scene. And when they climbed Vulture Peak together or visited Vaishali, the Buddha asked Ananda, "Vulture Peak is beautiful, is it not, Ananda?" "Isn't Vaishali beautiful, Ananda?" Details like these are found in the texts and show us that the Buddha never repudiated the joy and happiness of a peaceful mind or said that joy and happiness are obstacles to the practice. Wholesome feelings of joy and happiness can nourish the well-being of our body and mind and help us go far on the path of practice. Siddhartha gave up the practice of self-mortification after he remembered the joy he had experienced while meditating under a rose-apple tree as a young boy. We all need joy and happiness. We only have to be aware that all things are impermanent and subject to change, including the cool breeze, the setting sun, Vulture Peak, and Vaishali.

But the Buddha did speak of the five sense pleasures (money, sex, fame, overeating, and sleeping too much) as obstacles to the practice. If we get a reasonable amount of sleep every night, that cannot harm our practice. In fact, deep and refreshing sleep will help our practice. But if we spend a large part of each day sleeping, that is an obstacle. Joy and happiness, in this case, have become an indulgence in a sense pleasure. In the same way, a simple, well-prepared, nourishing meal, eaten slowly and mindfully so that we remain in deep contact with the food, is not an obstacle to the practice. But an obsession with food, spending much of our time seeking special foods, is an obstacle to the practice. Again, this is to turn the joy and happiness of a peaceful mind into an indulgence. The same is true of the remaining three sense pleasures — if we are caught or obsessed by them, they will present obstacles on our path of practice.

It is possible that Bhikshu Arittha was unable to draw a line between the joy and happiness of a peaceful mind and indulging in sense pleasures. If that is the case, he may just have been trying to express the idea that feelings of joy are not harmful for the practice. We know that he himself had never broken the most grave precepts, such as the precept forbidding a monk to have sexual intercourse, because we read in the *Vinaya* that he was not subjected by the Sangha to the penalty for breaking a *parajika* ("defeat") precept, which is permanent expulsion from the Sangha. He was only suspended temporarily for a less grave offense.

The bhikshus in Chabbaggiya were unable to persuade Bhikshu Arittha to give up his wrong view, perhaps because they were not able to explain clearly enough the difference between the joy and happiness of a peaceful mind and indulging in sense pleasures. They disciplined him, trying to get him to give up his view by finding him guilty of an offense. But, apparently, he never really submitted, as we read that a number of bhikshus and one bhikshuni stayed with him during his time of suspension, and, as a result, they were also suspended.

In the end, a number of monks from Chabbaggiya had to go to the Jeta Grove near Shravasti to report this matter to the Buddha. Arittha's attitude and misunderstanding were probably shared by some other members of the Chabbaggiya Sangha. It is regrettable that the sutra does not tell us more about Arittha's ideas, apart from his idea that "sense pleasures are not an obstacle to the practice."

5
SENSE PLEASURES AS DISASTERS

The disasters that, according to this sutra, are brought about by indulging in sense pleasures, are also listed in many other sutras: (1) Sense pleasures are a skeleton, bare bones thrown to a hungry dog that do nothing to appease its hunger. We do not receive nourishment or lasting contentment from indulging in sense pleasures. (2) Sense pleasures are a piece of raw flesh, a piece of waste meat of a butchered animal that a bird might pick up in its beak. If the bird does not let go of it when a larger bird comes along, there will be a fight and the smaller bird may be killed. Sense pleasures, in this sense, can kill us. (3) Sense pleasures are a burning torch. Its flame might burn the hand of the person holding the torch if the wind shifts suddenly. (4) Sense pleasures are a pit of burning charcoal into which we may be pushed and burn to death. (5) Sense pleasures are a poisonous snake, dangerous beyond measure. (6) Sense pleasures are a dream, short-lived and not real. (7) Sense pleasures are borrowed possessions. They do not belong to us, and we cannot hold on to them. (8) Sense pleasures are a tree laden with fruit. Its leaves and branches will be destroyed by those who come to pick the fruit. (9) Sense pleasures are an impaling stick, a sharp weapon that pierces the flesh. (10) Sense pleasures are a slaughterhouse, a place where lives are lost.

The idea that sense pleasures are a disaster and an obstacle to the practice must have been quite familiar to the bhikshus and bhikshunis. When we are obsessed by sense pleasures, we lose our freedom. This was taught by the Buddha, and it is also why we need the precepts to protect us from getting caught in sense pleasures. But we have to distinguish between indulging in sense pleasures and the joy and happiness that we experience when we are mindful and at peace. Indulging in sense pleasures is harmful, but enjoying peace and happiness is absolutely necessary for our physical and spiritual well-being, and for our practice on the path. Sense pleasures can bring about suffering and entanglement — both in the present moment and the future, for ourselves and others. The joy and happiness of a peaceful mind bring neither suffering nor attachment in the present or in the future, for ourselves or others. We practitioners need to develop our capacity for peace and joy if we want to realize the fruits of the practice. Nirvana is the highest peace and joy we can attain. If we practice only grimly and austerely, we will not be able to handle the peace and joy of nirvana. In the *Sutra on Knowing the Better Way to Catch a Snake,* the Buddha says that the Tathagata is a noble, cool, and fresh state, free of the discomfort of heat or sorrow. This is the state of nirvana.

6
THE DANGER OF MISUNDERSTANDING THE TEACHINGS

Arittha must have heard the Buddha talk about the joy and happiness of a mind at peace, but he seems not to have understood the difference between indulging in sense pleasures and the joy and happiness of a peaceful mind. We shouldn't think Bhikshu Arittha was unique in this misunderstanding. It is probably the case that a number of other monks also did not see the difference between the joy and happiness of a peaceful mind and indulging in sense pleasures, although most of the others probably erred in the opposite direction, being afraid of both sense pleasures and the joy and happiness of a peaceful mind. Today there are still practitioners of Buddhism who are afraid of joy and happiness, who do not dare to appreciate the beautiful and wonderful things of life because they have heard that all things are impermanent and contain suffering. They are even afraid to appreciate the beauty of a newly blossomed flower or a magnificent sunset, although they could do so in the full awareness that things are impermanent, subject to suffering, and without a separate self. Bhikshu Arittha must have come into contact with monks who had attitudes like this, and, unable to draw the line between indulging in sense pleasures and the joy and happiness of a peaceful mind, he went to the other extreme, saying that sense pleasures are not an obstacle to the practice. Because he went too far, the Buddha had to correct him.

The Buddha taught, *"Monks, it is important to understand my teachings thoroughly before you teach or put them into practice. If you have not understood the meaning of any teaching I give, please ask me or one of the elder brothers in the Dharma or one of the others who is excellent in the practice about it."* "Elder brothers in the Dharma" are those who have realized the practice and not those who simply have a vast store of knowledge. "Excellent in the practice" is a translation of *brahmacharya,* which means those whose lives are exemplary, pure, and clear. It does not mean those who live a harsh, austere life.

There are two reasons why someone might understand a teaching of the Buddha in the opposite way to which it was intended. One is the lack of insight or skillfulness due to inaccurately perceiving the letter or the spirit of the teachings. The other is a motivation that focuses on being able to win disputes or enhance one's reputation. Those who study the sutras in order to win arguments have lost sight that the practice is intended to be liberating. But this is not to suggest that all who study the sutras with a view to liberation are on the right path. They may be going in the right direction, but they still need insight and skillfulness if they are to understand the meaning of the sutra. Without insight and skill, they too will *"endure difficulties that are not of much benefit, and eventually exhaust themselves."* The Buddha taught, *"If you practice intelligently, you will understand both the letter and the spirit of the teachings and will be able to explain them correctly. Do not practice just to show off or argue with others. Practice to attain liberation, and if you do, you will have little pain or exhaustion."*

Skillfulness in receiving the letter and the spirit of the teachings without distorting the meaning is the correct way to study the Dharma. Here skillfulness is accompanied by intelligence, and the meaning of intelligence is understanding. Without skill and intelligence, we can easily misunderstand the teachings.

7

CATCHING A SNAKE

At this point, the Buddha presents the simile of catching a snake. He says that a skillful, intelligent snake catcher always uses a forked stick to pin the snake just below the head so that the snake cannot turn around and bite him. This comparison is extremely apt:

"Bhikshus, a person who studies that way can be compared to a man trying to catch a poisonous snake in the wild. If he reaches out his hand, the snake may bite his hand, leg, or some other part of his body. Trying to catch a snake that way has no advantages and can only create suffering.

"Bhikshus, understanding my teaching in the wrong way is the same. If you do not practice the Dharma correctly, you may come to understand it as the opposite of what was intended. But if you practice intelligently, you will understand both the letter and the spirit of the teachings and will be able to explain them correctly. Do not practice just to show off or argue with others. Practice to attain liberation, and if you do, you will have little pain or exhaustion.

"Bhikshus, an intelligent student of the Dharma is like a man who uses a forked stick to catch a snake. When he sees a poisonous snake in the wild, he places the stick right below the head of the snake and grabs the snake's neck with his hand. Even if the snake winds itself around the man's hand, leg, or another part of his body, it will not bite him. This is the better way to catch a snake, and it will not lead to pain or exhaustion.

"Bhikshus, a son or daughter of good family who studies the Dharma needs to apply the utmost skill to understanding the letter and the spirit of the teachings. He or she should not study with the aim of boasting, debating, or arguing, but only to attain liberation. Studying in this way, with intelligence, he or she will have little pain or exhaustion."

There are probably not many teachers who would compare their own teachings to a poisonous snake. There must not be many who would say that their teachings can be dangerous if not understood and practiced correctly. The Buddha never said that his teachings were the absolute truth. He called them skillful means to guide us in the practice. The way to make use of these teachings is with our own intelligence and skill.

The Buddha described himself at other times as a doctor whose teachings are a kind of medicine. If the medicine is used correctly, it can help cure sickness. But if it is misused, it can threaten a patient's life. We have accounts of several occasions during the Buddha's lifetime in which his teachings were misunderstood and practiced incorrectly. During one rainy-season retreat, in the great forest near Vaishali, a number of monks took their own lives after hearing teachings on the foulness of the body, impermanence, no-self, and emptiness. These bhikshus heard the teachings from the Buddha and yet completely misunderstood the meaning. If it is possible to hear the teachings from the Buddha himself and still misconstrue them, how much more dangerous it is for those of us who are hearing the teachings after many centuries of oral and written transmission and interpretation. We have to use our own skill and intelligence to determine the Buddha's true intention in offering any teaching, and we must be humble when we do.

8

THE RAFT IS NOT THE SHORE

The snake simile is used to convey the danger we risk when we study the sutras without skill and intelligence. In the *Sutra on Knowing the Better Way to Catch a Snake,* there is another excellent simile, that of the raft. It shows how we can get caught by the teachings.

"Bhikshus, I have told you many times the importance of knowing when it is time to let go of a raft and not hold onto it unnecessarily. When a mountain stream overflows and becomes a torrent of floodwater carrying debris, a man or woman who wants to get across might think, 'What is the safest way to cross this floodwater?' Assessing the situation, she may decide to gather branches and grasses, construct a raft, and use it to cross to the other side. But, after arriving on the other side, she thinks, 'I spent a lot of time and energy building this raft. It is a prized possession, and I will carry it with me as I continue my journey.' If she puts it on her shoulders or head and carries it with her on land, bhikshus, do you think that would be intelligent?"

The bhikshus replied, "No, World-Honored One."

The Buddha said, "How could she have acted more wisely? She could have thought, 'This raft helped me get across the water safely. Now I will leave it at the water's edge for someone else to use in the same way.' Wouldn't that be a more intelligent thing to do?"

The bhikshus replied, "Yes, World-Honored One."

The Buddha taught, "I have given this teaching on the raft many times to remind you how necessary it is to let go of all the true teachings, not to mention teachings that are not true."

"It is necessary to let go of all the true teachings, not to mention teachings that are not true." This mighty proclamation can be compared to the roar of a lion. The same proclamation is made in its entirety in the *Vajracchedika Prajñaparamita Sutra (Diamond That Cuts through Illusion)*. This lion's roar has the power to help the practitioner give up the attitude of clinging even if he or she has had it for many thousands of lifetimes. The shout of Ch'an Master Lin Chi is simply the echo of this lion's roar of the Buddha. The Buddha teaches impermanence, no-self, emptiness, and nirvana not as theories, but as skillful means to help us in our practice. If we take these teachings and use them as theories, we will be trapped. In the time of the Buddha and also today, many people study Buddhism only in view of satisfying the thirst of their intellect. They pride themselves on their understanding of Buddhist systems of thought and use them in debates and discussions as a kind of game or amusement. It is quite different from a Dharma discussion, when we discuss the teachings with co-practitioners in order to shed light on the path of practice.

The teachings of impermanence, no-self, and emptiness were offered by the Buddha to help us liberate ourselves from our psychological prisons and pains. If someone studies and practices these teachings and does not find release from attachment and pain, he or she has not understood the letter and spirit of these teachings. He or she is caught in the form and has not been in touch with the substance. The simile of the raft is offered to help us see what it is to be caught in form. Instead of just using the raft to transport ourselves and others across the river, we want to carry it with us on our head or shoulders. Just as a raft that is not used to carry people is not performing its proper function, teachings that are used for speculative purposes are not able to release people from their sufferings and attachments. Teachings received in the wrong way are, as the sutra says, "teachings that are not true" (or "non-teachings," in Chinese, *fei fa*). True teachings can be used as a raft to cross the river; teachings that are not true cannot. Being caught in the true teachings is harmful enough. Being caught by the teachings that are not true is much worse. With teachings that are not true, we can never arrive at the other shore. Anyone who has arrived at the other shore has used the raft of true teachings, and he or she is advised not to be attached to the raft. We must be free even from true teachings, not to mention non-teachings. This is the meaning of the parable. Even if we undertake the crossing, if we are attached to what we learn, we have not understood it properly, and we have been bitten by the snake. In this case, a true raft is not available to us, and therefore we cannot cross the river. We may not even realize the importance of crossing to the other shore. The sutra warns us against this.

Nirvana is the release from the prisons of attachment, above all from the attachment to ideas, including ideas of impermanence, no-self, emptiness, and nirvana. In the *Maharatnakuta Sutra*, the Buddha says: "It is better to be caught in the idea that everything exists than to be caught in the idea of emptiness. Someone who is caught in the idea that everything exists can still be disentangled, but it is difficult to disentangle someone who is caught in the idea of emptiness." This is also true of the teachings of impermanence, no-self, nirvana, and every other teaching. All teachings are offered as skillful means to help us along on the path. They are not absolute truth. If we do not know how to use these teachings skillfully, we will be enslaved by them. Instead of helping us, they will only cause us harm. If we put our raft on our shoulders as we walk, we will only strain ourselves and, when we are ready to cross over to the other shore or make our raft available to others, we will not be able to do so.

9

THE FINGER POINTING AT THE MOON

The *Surangama Sutra* (*Taisho* 945) tells us, "If someone uses a finger to point out the moon to another person, if that person takes the finger to be the moon, he will not only fail to see the moon, but he will also fail to see the finger." The *Lankavatara Sutra* (*Taisho* 640) says, "All the teachings in the sutras are fingers pointing to the moon." These pointing fingers are not the moon itself, just as the raft is not the other shore. The teachings of the Buddha are not in themselves the experience of enlightenment, just as a map of Paris is not the city of Paris itself.

Master Tai Hsu, a well-known Chinese teacher of the 1920s and 1930s, distinguished between "essence teachings" and "image teachings." The former are the essence of enlightenment, the Buddha's realization under the Bodhi tree that cannot be expressed in words or concepts. When the Buddha began teaching in the Deer Park, image teachings were given, and these belong to the realms of concepts and spoken words. Image teachings are a shadow of the truth; they are not truth itself. If we study the image teachings and see that they are just shadows, they can help us touch the essence teachings, just as we can follow a tree's shadow to find and touch the tree itself.

10
THE PHEASANT

In the *Sutra of One Hundred Parables* (*Taisho* 209), the Buddha tells a story about words and concepts. A foolish man became ill, and when the doctor came to see him, he said that only pheasant could cure his disease. After the doctor left, the patient repeated the word "pheasant" hour after hour and day after day. Months passed, but he still was not cured. One day, a friend came to visit, and hearing the man repeat the word "pheasant" over and over, asked him why. The sick man told him what the doctor had said, and taking pity on him, his friend took a pencil and drew a pheasant. He showed it to the foolish man and told him, "This is what a pheasant looks like. You have to eat it if you want to cure your disease. Just repeating the word 'pheasant' is not enough." As soon as his friend left, the foolish man put the drawing of the pheasant in his mouth, chewed, and swallowed it. When he did not get well as a result of this, he hired an artist to draw hundreds more pheasants, and he chewed and swallowed all of them, but his illness only worsened, and, eventually, he contacted the doctor again.

When the doctor saw what had happened, great pity welled up in him. He took the foolish man's hand and walked with him to the market. There he bought two pheasants, accompanied the man home, helped him prepare them for eating, and asked the man to eat them before his eyes. After that, the foolish man was cured.

When we hear this story, we may think how incredibly stupid that man was. But when we look more deeply, we may see that we ourselves are not much better. Because we lack intelligence and skill, we study the Dharma and discuss it for amusement or merely to show off. We are not determined enough to liberate ourselves from our deepest suffering. We remain attached to words and ideas, both in our study and our practice. The way we count our breaths, practice loving kindness meditation, or recite mantras can also lack in intelligence and skill. We can get caught in the forms. It is not easy to give rise to awakened understanding.

11

BREAKING THE BONDS

The *Sutra on Knowing the Better Way to Catch a Snake* does not aim at expounding the harm of sense pleasures or explaining concepts of no-self, nirvana, or tathagata, although the sutra does mention these concepts. The main purpose of the sutra is to demonstrate the necessity of breaking the bonds of attachment. The Buddha shows us why it is a hindrance to be attached to anything, including his own teachings. That is why he says to "let go of all the true teachings, not to mention teachings that are not true." This is the quintessence of this sutra and of all Buddhist teachings. The word translated as "teachings" in this sentence is "Dharma." This spirit — this way of breaking through the bonds of attachment — is the foremost element of the Buddhist teachings.

Breaking the bonds of attachment is the most skillful and intelligent way to practice. We study the Dharma to understand and practice it, not to accumulate knowledge. Knowledge not used skillfully is an obstacle to understanding. "Knowledge" in Sanskrit is *jñeya* ("the object to be known"). Obstacles produced by our knowing something are called *jñeya avarana.* We might call them prejudices or obstinacy. If we can let go of our knowledge, we are free to reach a deeper understanding. It is like climbing a ladder — if we cannot let go of the fifth rung, we will never be able to step up to the sixth. If we think that the fifth rung is the highest rung possible, this will be the end of our climbing. This attitude is an obstacle produced by knowledge.

In the *Sutra of One Hundred Parables,* the Buddha tells this story. One day, while a young father was absent from his home in a rural village, a band of robbers came, stole all of the villagers' possessions, burned their houses to the ground, and kidnapped all the children, including his son. When the father returned to the village, he was stricken with grief. Seeing the charred corpse of a child in the ashes of what had been his house, he wept, beat his chest, and performed funeral rites for his son. Then he put the ashes into an embroidered pouch, which he carried around his neck wherever he went. Some months later, after the village had been completely rebuilt, the man's son was able to escape from the robbers and find his way home. That night, at about midnight, he knocked on his father's door, but the father, holding the pouch with the ashes, his face bathed in tears, was determined not to let the boy in. The child told him his name, but the man was certain that his son had been killed and that the boy at the door must be mocking his grief. In the end, the boy had to give up, and father and son were separated forever. If we are caught by the obstacle of knowledge, even if truth comes knocking at our door, we will refuse to let it in.

12

THUNDERING SILENCE

In the *Samyutta Nikaya,* we read about the ascetic Vacchagotta's visit to the Buddha. Vacchagotta asked, "Reverend Gautama, please tell me, is there a self?" The Buddha did not say anything. Vacchagotta asked again, "Then you do not think there is a self?" The Buddha remained silent. Eventually, Vacchagotta left.

Afterwards, Ananda asked the Buddha, "Venerable Sir, when you give us Dharma teachings you often speak about no-self. Why did you not reply to Vacchagotta's questions concerning the self?" The Buddha replied, "The teaching of no-self that I give the bhikshus is a means to guide you to look deeply in your meditation. It is not an ideology. If you make it into an ideology, you will be caught in it. I believe the ascetic Vacchagotta was looking for an ideology and not for a teaching to help him in the practice. So I remained silent. I did not want him to be caught by the teachings. If I had told him there is a self, that would not have been correct. If I told him there is no self, he would have clung to that dogmatically and made it into a theory, and that would not have been helpful either. That is why I kept silent."

In the *Vimalakirti Nirdesha Sutra* (*Taisho* 475), the silence of the layman Vimalakirti is praised by the Bodhisattva Mañjushri as a "thundering silence" that echoes far and wide, having the power to break the bonds of attachment and bring about liberation. It is the same as the lion's roar that proclaims, "It is necessary to let go of all the true teachings, not to mention teachings that are not true." This is the spirit we need if we want to understand the *Sutra on Knowing the Better Way to Catch a Snake*.

The first precept of the Order of Interbeing represents the same spirit: "Do not be idolatrous about or bound to any doctrine, theory, or ideology, even Buddhist ones. Buddhist systems of thought are guiding means; they are not absolute truth." Teachings that are received as doctrines or theories are no longer teachings. They do not liberate, and the person receiving them is caught. In most precept texts, the first precept is not to take life. Not taking life, however, is not unique to Buddhism. In the Jainism of the naked ascetic Nirgantha, for example, restrictions concerning the taking of life were far more severe than in Buddhism. But in the spirit of breaking the bonds of attachment to ideology, the practice of the precept not to kill goes much further in Buddhism. A person caught in a doctrine or a system of thought can sacrifice millions of lives in order to put into practice his theory, which he considers the absolute truth, the unique path that can lead humankind to happiness. With a gun in hand, a person can kill one, five, or even ten people. But holding on to a doctrine or a system of thought, one can kill tens of thousands of people. Therefore, unless the precept not to take life is understood in terms of breaking the bonds of attachment to ideology, it is not truly the precept taught by the Buddha.

13

NO-SELF

The teaching of no-self is one of the teachings of Buddhism most likely to be misunderstood. The Buddha refers to this teaching in the *Sutra on Knowing the Better Way to Catch a Snake* as an example of how many people have misunderstood his teachings, including brahmans. There is a simple and general way to explain no-self, which is that there is no single entity whose identity is changeless. All things are constantly changing. Nothing endures forever or contains a changeless element called a "self."

The Buddha refers to the six bases of views that are the ground for the idea of a self. "Ground" means the place in which we can take refuge, and when we take refuge in views, the term "view-refuge" is also used (Pali: *ditthi-nissaya*). The six bases are form (the body), feelings, perceptions (or ideas), mental formations, consciousness, and the world. The Buddha taught in many of his discourses, "The body, whether a body of the past, a body in the present moment, whether it is our own body or someone else's, subtle or gross, whether beautiful or ugly, near or far, is not mine, is not me, is not the self. A practitioner should meditate on this to be able to see the truth concerning a body."

The Buddha taught that there are three categories of wrong view of self: (1) *This body is mine.* This means that we see the body not as ourselves but as something that belongs to us, with an independent existence outside of, or apart from, ourselves. (2) *This body is me.* This body and I are one. This body is exactly the same as me. (3) *This body is the Self.* This body is the *Atman,* a spiritual first principle, a basic constituent of the universe present in every species and every thing. The body is not the possession of a separate, individual self, or one and the same as a separate, individual self. It is the spiritual essence of the whole universe.

In the Buddha's lifetime there were many theories concerning the self. Both Vedic and Upanishadic literature speak about it in various ways. In ancient Brahmanism, we find a belief similar to pantheism. According to this point of view, the Self (Atman) is found everywhere and Brahman is the permanent and absolute element at the beginning and end of everything in the universe. Sometimes Brahman is called "Great Self" *(Mahatman)* or "True Self" *(Paratman).* Within every species and every individual there is a piece of this Great Self that can be called "self" or "small self." This element is unchanging and absolute. It is not born and does not die. Liberation takes place when this small "self" returns to and merges with the Great Self. This is an oversimplification, but it conveys the essence of this belief. In Vedic and Upanishadic literature there are many more theories about the self, some quite complex. The *Brahmajala Sutta (Digha Nikaya,* Sutta No. 1) deals with sixty-three of these. When the Buddha proclaims that this body is not the self, it must be understood in the context of the Brahmanic beliefs of his time.

This body is not mine, is not me, and is not the self. These feelings are not mine, are not me, and are not the self. The same is true of perceptions, mental formations, and consciousness. Each aggregate of personality is like that, and the Five Aggregates combined are also like that.

"*Whatever we see, hear, perceive, know, mentally grasp, observe, or think about at the present time or any other time is not ours, is not us, is not the self.*" After discussing the selfless nature of the fifth aggregate, consciousness, the Buddha goes on to discuss the sixth ground of views, the world: "*Some people think, 'The world is the self. The self is the world. The world is me. I will continue to exist without changing even after I die. I am eternal. I will never disappear.' Please meditate so you can see that the world is not mine, is not me, is not the self. Please look deeply so you can see the truth concerning the world.*"

It is very clear from this quotation that the Buddha is referring to the Brahmanic belief in the self as the basic, unchanging, unfading constituent of the universe. In the *Brahmajala Sutta,* the Buddha says, "There are ascetics and brahmans who belong to the school of thought professing eternalism, which holds that the self and the universe are one — permanent and unchanging *(sassatavada sassatam attanañca lokañca paññapenti).*"

Usually it is enough for the Buddha to speak of five grounds only, the Five Aggregates of personality, because according to the Buddhist way of seeing things the world is all included within the Five Aggregates. The world is an object of consciousness, and, therefore, it is consciousness. An object of consciousness is called a dharma, and all dharmas constitute the world. The reason the Buddha adds the sixth ground here is to have an opportunity to discuss in detail being caught in the view of an Atman as the spiritual basis of the whole universe. In the Pali version of the *Sutra on Knowing the Better Way to Catch a Snake,* we read "*so loko, so atto...*" which literally means "This is the world, this is the self." This can also be understood as, "The world is the self, the self is the world."

In the S*utra on the Sign of No-Self* (*Anattalakkhana Sutta, Samyutta Nikaya,* Vol. III, p. 66), the second discourse the Buddha gave after his enlightenment, it is taught that because there is not a self, the Five Aggregates of personality are not enduring and do not have sovereignty. Our Five Aggregates may want to be eternal, unchanging, and beautiful, but they cannot be as our mind wants them to be. This is one of the ways of explaining the teaching on no-self. In the same sutra, the Buddha also says, "Bhikshus, the body is not self. If the body were self, it would not be a cause of afflictions and we could say to the body, 'You should be like this,' or 'You should not be like this.' The same is true of the other four aggregates of personality: feelings, perceptions, mental formations, and consciousness." In this passage, the Buddha is thinking about self as an absolute entity with sovereignty. Because there is no sovereignty within the Five Aggregates of personality, it can be said that there is no self present within the Five Aggregates of personality.

14
DITTHI-NISSAYA (VIEW-REFUGE)

To establish peace of mind, to be free of the fear of annihilation (nihilism), human beings tend to cling to the idea of a self. This is a universal human need. Even the busiest person cannot avoid reflecting on the matter of life and death once in a while. Perhaps our death will be sudden and unexpected, or perhaps it will be prolonged. Will we just turn into nothingness? Because we human beings are afraid of nothingness, we cling to the belief in a permanent, indestructible self. Sometimes we look for explanations why there must be a self. "I think, therefore I am," Descartes' position, is an expression of this need.

We also have a need to identify the self with something, whether it is the body, feelings, perceptions, mental formations, consciousness, or the world. Believing that the world will last forever, that the world is the self, and that the self will persist with the world are ways of clinging to the self. According to the teachings of Buddhism, everything is impermanent. The Five Aggregates are impermanent and the world is also impermanent. To look for an eternal self is a fruitless endeavor, like taking refuge in a sand castle. Sooner or later, sand castles must collapse, and, in the end, searching for an eternal self only brings us anxiety, exhaustion, sorrow, suffering, and despair. Let us read this passage from the *Sutra on Knowing the Better Way to Catch a Snake:*

"Bhikshus, do you think the Five Aggregates and the self are permanent, changeless, and not subject to destruction?"

"No, reverend teacher."

"Is there anything you can hold on to with attachment that will not cause anxiety, exhaustion, sorrow, suffering, and despair?"

"No, reverend teacher."

"Is there any view of self in which you can take refuge that will not cause anxiety, exhaustion, sorrow, suffering, and despair?"

"No, reverend teacher."

A place where one takes refuge in a view of self is called, in Pali, ditthi-nissaya, "view-refuge." As long as we continue to take refuge in views, we continue to experience fear, suffering, and despair. Therefore, it is best to give up all view-

refuges. To believe in an eternal self is fruitless and dangerous. When one day we lose that belief for one reason or another, we will plummet into the depths of confusion and despair. From the extreme of being caught in a view of the self as eternal, we will fall into the abyss of nihilism, the other extreme, and our suffering and confusion will be boundless. The following passage from the sutra refers to this danger:

Upon hearing this, one bhikshu stood up, bared his right shoulder, joined his palms respectfully, and asked the Buddha, "World-Honored One, can fear and anxiety arise from an internal source?"

The Buddha replied, "Yes, fear and anxiety can arise from an internal source. If you think, 'Things that did not exist in the past have come to exist, but now no longer exist,' you will feel sad or become confused and despairing. This is how fear and anxiety can arise from an internal source."

"Things" refers to the self: "In the past, before my mother gave birth to me, I did not exist. After my mother gave birth to me, naturally I existed. I believed I existed. Despite that, today I see that I do not exist. I am nothing at all." This is to go from being caught in existence to being caught in nonexistence, from being caught in permanence to being caught in nihilism. These are all extreme views. The insight of the Buddha goes beyond these extremes so that we remain in the Middle Way, which is neither existence nor nonexistence, permanence nor annihilation.

"Things" here are the self to which we cling. (To explain "things" as the material offerings that are made to the bhikshus, as one commentator suggested, is not correct, and indicates that the author has caught the snake by the wrong end.) "Things" could also be the belief in a soul or in heaven. Without such a belief, we may feel confused, and with it, we may feel comfort, so we cling to that belief. But our clinging is also accompanied by anxiety or longing, and if some day we experience upheaval or loss, our faith will be undermined and our suffering will be unbearable. We will "feel sad and become completely confused and despairing." The Buddha asks, "Is there anything you can hold on to with attachment that will not cause anxiety, exhaustion, sorrow, suffering, and despair?"

15
THE WAY TO PRACTICE THE TEACHINGS OF NO-SELF

When we realize the true nature of no-self, we can let go of all of the grounds of view. We no longer need to cling to or identify ourselves with anything, and we will no longer fall into states of confusion, anxiety, or sorrow. To receive the teachings of no-self requires us to use our full intelligence and skillfulness. If we do not, these same teachings can cause us confusion, anxiety, and sorrow, especially during times of upheaval and loss in our lives. If we receive the teachings of no-self incorrectly, we may think they are about nihilism and destruction, and feelings of despair may overwhelm us. If we believe the world is a self, that we are that self, and that we will endure as long as the world endures, when we hear the Buddhist teaching of no-self and we are not ready for it, we will immediately fall into a state of confusion. From being caught in a view that everything exists, we will descend into a view that nothing exists. From being caught in a view that everything is permanent, we will descend into a view that everything is nonexistent. Even though the teachings on no-self are not theories of nihilism or destruction, if we receive them as if they were, we have caught the snake by the tail. A brahman could fall into this condition. From his belief in self, he could descend into the confusion of nihilism and nonbeing:

"World-Honored One, can fear and anxiety arise from an external source?"

The Buddha taught, "Fear and anxiety can arise from an external source. You may think, 'This is a self. This is the world. This is myself. I will exist forever.' Then if you meet the Buddha or a disciple of the Buddha who has the understanding and intelligence to teach you how to let go of all views of attachment to the body, the self, and the objects of the self with a view to giving up pride, internal formations, and energy leaks, and you think, 'This is the end of the world. I have to give up everything. I am not the world. I am not me. I am not a self. I will not exist forever. When I die, I will be completely annihilated. There is nothing to look forward to, to be joyful about, or to remember,' you will feel sad and become confused and despairing. This is how fear and anxiety can arise from an external source."

We can lose faith in the presence of a self for reasons that are within ourselves, and when we hear the teachings of no-self, we can lose that faith for reasons that are outside ourselves. If we lose faith in the self from hearing the teachings, we are like one who is bitten by a snake while trying to catch it. This is the theme of this sutra.

Reading the sutra this far, we understand how many people have misunderstood the teachings of no-self. We have learned that among the Five Aggregates of personality and the world, there is nothing that is not subject to change.

But we should note that the Buddha never taught that the Five Aggregates and the world are nonexisting. The coming together of the Five Aggregates is an existence, although it is an impermanent and selfless existence. This existence is impermanent and selfless, therefore in its essence it cannot be described as being or not being, eternal or subject to annihilation. The Five Aggregates and the world transcend the four categories of being *(bhava),* nonbeing *(abhava),* permanence *(sassata),* and annihilation *(uccheda).* This is the Buddha's teaching of the Middle Way. It is offered in many sutras of both the Northern and Southern traditions. The following passage from the *Sutra on the Middle Way* elucidates this point:

"When someone observes the coming-to-be of the world, he is not caught in the idea that the world does not exist. When someone observes the fading away of the world, he is not caught in the idea that the world exists. Kaccayana, in the world there are two extreme views: the view of being and the view of nonbeing. The Tathagata is not caught by either view. He teaches the Dharma of the Middle Way." (*Samyukta Agama,* Sutra No. 301, equivalent to *Kaccanagotta Sutta, Samyutta Nikaya,* Vol. II, pp. 16–17.)

16
THE NON-ACHIEVED AND THE NON-EXPRESSED

In the *Sutra on Knowing the Better Way to Catch a Snake,* the teachings on no-self are described in the context of the brahmanic belief of Self (Atman). Within the Buddhist community, the Buddha usually spoke of self in terms of the three different ways of being caught in the view of self: (1) self (me, I), (2) object of self (mine), and (3) self within something or something within self. To understand this, let us look at the example of the body:

1. *I am this body.* We identify our self with our body. "I am the body. The body is me."

2. *This body is mine.* I and the body are not identical. The body is my possession, like my name, my belongings, or my bank account.

3. *I am in this body, this body is in me.* The body is not me, but I am present in the body. I am not the body, but the body is in me. The self lies in the body and the body lies in the self. In Chinese this is called *xiang zai,* "mutual inter-containing." This view is the most subtle and is linked to the idea, developed by a few later Buddhist schools, that the self is not the Five Aggregates, but without the Five Aggregates, the self cannot exist.

These three categories (of being caught in the view of self) are mentioned in many sutras, especially in the *Samyukta Agama* and the *Samyutta Nikaya.* They are three traps we may fall into. When we are free of the first two traps, we may still fall into the third, which is more subtle. Among Buddhists in many traditions, there are always people looking for a ground of views so they can establish a subtle sense of self, because, as we have already seen, the need to cling to a self is a powerful one. The *Sutra on Knowing the Better Way to Catch a Snake* is unique in that it mentions the sixth ground of views, "the world is self," which is a fourth trap, after the view of xiang zai, or mutual inter-containing. The Buddha teaches that the idea of "I" or "me" arises on the basis of the idea of "mine," and the idea of "mine" arises on the basis of the idea of "I" or "me." Both are wrong perceptions, with no basis, so they cannot be established or grasped. If we try to establish and hold on to an idea of self, we just bring suffering and despair on ourselves. Thus the four traps, or ways of establishing a self, are only a smoke screen of wrong perceptions — internal formations that are responsible for our present and future suffering.

This is the Buddha's teaching:

"Whenever there is an idea of self, there is also an idea of what belongs to the self. When there is no idea of self, there is no idea of anything that belongs to the self. Self and what belongs to the self are two views that are based on trying to grasp things that cannot be grasped, and to establish things that cannot be established. Such wrong perceptions cause us to be bound by internal formations that arise the moment we are caught by ideas that cannot be grasped or established and have no basis in reality."

The Five Aggregates and the world have their own suchness. Our ideas about the Five Aggregates arise within the framework of notions of existence, nonexistence, permanence, destruction, and so on. These notions cannot contain or hold reality, just as a net cannot contain or hold space. That is what is meant by "cannot be grasped" and "cannot be established." Such teachings are important in Buddhism. The Sanskrit term for "ungraspable" is *anupalabhya*. Here it is translated as "cannot be grasped" and "cannot be established." Despite the inestimable importance of this teaching, it was never developed to its fullest by either the Sarvastivada or Tamrashatiya schools of Buddhism.

17
NIRVANA

Nirvana is another teaching that is easily misunderstood. The basic meaning of nirvana is "extinction," or "to blow out a flame." It means to blow out the flame of afflictions, suffering, and hatred. It also means the extinction of ideas of existence, nonexistence, permanence, destruction, impermanence, no-self, Middle Way, ungraspable, samsara, and even nirvana itself. In spite of this, many people continue to understand nirvana as a state of nothingness and annihilation. The snake of the teachings on nirvana is frequently grasped by the tail.

In the *Sutra on Knowing the Better Way to Catch a Snake* we read, *"If, when he considers the six bases for wrong views, a bhikshu does not give rise to the idea of 'I' or 'mine,' he is not caught in the chains of this life. Since he is not caught in the chains of this life, he has no fear. To have no fear is to arrive at nirvana. Such a person is no longer troubled by birth and death; the holy life has been lived; what needs to be done has been done; there will be no further births or deaths; and the truth of things as they are is known."*

Here "nirvana" is defined as:

1. To have realized in practice the teachings of no-self (*"the holy life has been lived; what needs to be done has been done"*).

2. To arrive at right understanding (*"the truth of things as they are is known"*).

3. To be able to put an end to the cycle of birth and death (*"Such a person is no longer troubled by birth and death"*).

4. To have no fear (*"he has no fear"*).

After defining nirvana, the Buddha says a little more about its characteristics: *"Such a bhikshu has filled in the moat, crossed the moat, destroyed the enemy citadel, unbolted the door, and is able to look directly into the mirror of highest understanding.*" Here nirvana is described as a struggle for liberation, a victory, and the complete satisfaction of the one who has arrived at full understanding.

Let us read on:

"*What is meant by 'filling in the moat'? 'Filling in the moat' means to know and clearly understand the substance of ignorance. Ignorance has been uprooted and shattered and cannot arise anymore.*

"*What is meant by 'crossing the moat'? 'Crossing the moat' means to know and clearly understand the substance of becoming and craving. Becoming and craving have been uprooted and shattered and cannot arise anymore.*

"*What is meant by 'destroying the enemy citadel'? 'Destroying the enemy citadel' means to know and clearly understand the substance of the cycle of birth and death. The cycle of birth and death has been uprooted and shattered and cannot arise anymore.*

"*What is meant by 'unbolting the door'? 'Unbolting the door' means to know and clearly understand the substance of the five dull internal formations. The five dull internal formations have been uprooted and shattered and cannot arise anymore.*

"*What is meant by 'looking directly into the mirror of highest understanding'? 'Looking directly into the mirror of highest understanding' means to know and understand clearly the substance of pride. Pride has been uprooted and shattered and cannot arise anymore.*"

Pride is produced by being caught in a view of self. "Looking directly into the mirror of highest understanding" means liberation from being caught by a view of self.

18
TATHAGATA

Even though the Buddha described nirvana in very concrete terms, as above, he was often misunderstood, and nihilistic views and ideas of non-continuation were attributed to him. People misunderstood because they thought that once nirvana was attained, everything ceased to exist — that a leaf was no longer a leaf, a flower no longer a flower, a person no longer a person. Everything dissolved into empty space, losing all delineation. But the Buddha never said that nirvana was a huge gap of nothingness. To realize nirvana means not to be caught by ideas of birth and death, existence and non-existence, one and many, coming and going. Someone who abides in nirvana is a Tathagata.

The concept "tathagata" is deep and wonderful. This is not stressed or developed in the Sarvastivada and Tamrashatiya traditions. According to the *Vajracchedika Prajñaparamita Sutra* (*Taisho* 235), the Tathagata is someone who does not come from anywhere and does not go anywhere. Elsewhere, it is said that the Tathagata is one who comes from suchness and returns to suchness. This is another way of saying that the Tathagata does not come and does not go, because he or she realizes the path and abides in nirvana.

In the *Sutra on Knowing the Better Way to Catch a Snake*, the Buddha says, *"The Tathagata is a noble fount of freshness and coolness. There is no great heat and no sorrow in this state."* The Tathagata has the joy of peace, freedom, and happiness. The Tathagata, just like nirvana, cannot be confined to categories like birth and death, existence and nonexistence, one and many, coming and going. One will never find the Tathagata in concepts, even if the one searching is Indra, the king of the gods, Prajapati, or Brahma.

In the Mahayana scriptures, beginning with the *Prajña-paramita and Maharatnakuta Sutras* and continuing in the *Avatamsaka* and *Vimalakirti Nirdesha Sutras,* there is an effort to present the teachings of the Middle Way to help people not be caught in the ideas of nothingness and non-continuation. The *Madhyamaka Shastra,* by Nagarjuna, has the same aim when explaining the eight characteristics that are not the Middle Way: birth, death, permanence, non-continuation, oneness, otherness, coming, and going.

In the *Anuradha Sutta* (*Samyutta Nikaya,* Vol. III, pp. 116–119), a small group of wandering ascetics met the Bhikshu Anuradha and asked him whether, after death, the Tathagata (1) continues to exist, (2) ceases to exist, (3) both continues and ceases to exist, or (4) neither continues nor ceases to exist. Anuradha said that none of the four propositions expressed the truth about the Tathagata. The ascetics thought that he was either unintelligent or new to the practice, and they left him. When he returned to the monastery, Bhikshu Anuradha told the Buddha what had happened and asked for his response. The Buddha asked Anuradha if he could find the Tathagata in the body, feelings, perceptions, mental formations, or consciousness. The bhikshu replied that he could not. The Buddha asked him if he could find the Tathagata outside of the body, feelings, perceptions, mental formations, or consciousness, and Anuradha again said no. The Buddha said, "Bhikshu Anuradha, if you cannot find the Tathagata while the Tathagata is still here, how can you expect to find the Tathagata within these four propositions after he is dead?"

In the Chinese version of the *Sutra on Knowing the Better Way to Catch a Snake,* the Buddha says, "Indra, Prajapati, Brahma, and the other gods in their entourage, however hard they look, cannot find any trace or basis for the consciousness of a Tathagata." The Pali version states, "I say that right here and now it is impossible to find any trace of the Tathagata" *(ditth' ev' aham, bhikkhave, dhamme Tathagatam ananuvejjo 'ti vadami).* In the Pali version, the Buddha concludes, "In former times and still today, the Tathagata teaches only about suffering and the path to transform suffering." The Buddha did not want to waste time looking for ideas and categories of reality. He maintained that such a search could not be of help to anyone, and, in any case, no conclusion could be reached. The eight "no's"[16] of the Middle Way cited by Nagarjuna are already clearly expressed in these early Buddhist sutras.

So that people do not fall into the abyss of nothingness and non-continuation, the *Mahaparinirvana Sutra* says that permanence, joy, sovereignty, and purity are the four characteristics of nirvana. These four notions had been considered the four basic wrong perceptions, called the four perverted views, but we are taught otherwise in the *Mahaparinirvana Sutra* in order to heal ideas of nothingness and non-continuation, a kind of medicine to heal snakebites.

19

TREATING WRONG UNDERSTANDING

In every age and every place, there are people who misunderstand the teachings of the Buddha. How can one respond

---

[16] The eight "no's" are: no birth, no death, no permanence, no annihilation, no oneness, no otherness, no coming, no going.

to these kinds of misunderstandings? The Buddha addresses this in the last part of the sutra.

"*When recluses and brahmans hear me say this, they may slander me, saying that I do not speak the truth, that the monk Gautama proposes a theory of nihilism and teaches absolute nonexistence, while in fact living beings do exist. Bhikshus, the Tathagata has never taught the things they say.*" Although the Buddha said clearly that he did not support theories of nihilism and non-continuation, for 2,600 years there have always been people who accuse him of exactly that.

It is because the teachings of the Buddha are so deep that they are easily misunderstood. Although the Buddha never said that living beings do not exist, because of some of the things he did say, some people always understand him to be teaching that living beings do not exist. In the *Vajracchedika Prajñaparamita Sutra,* for example, the Buddha says, "If a bodhisattva thinks there really are sentient beings, he is not yet an authentic bodhisattva." Here, the Buddha was giving the teaching of no-self. In light of interdependent co-origination, sentient beings can only exist because of non-sentient species. To think that sentient beings can possibly exist in isolation from the non-sentient world is a mistake. The Buddha is trying to help us transcend the idea of an independent, separate living being, which is one of the four notions: self, living being, person, and life span. But he only had to open his mouth to be misunderstood. That is why in the Mahayana tradition, we hear this saying of the Buddha, "In forty-five years I have never said anything." It means, "Please do not get caught by any of my words." The Buddha's silent response to Vacchagotta's questions is the same.

How can we face people who falsely accuse, reprimand, or slander us? The Buddha suggests we practice the teaching of no-self. When we practice no-self, false accusations, reprimands, and slander cannot hurt us. When we are in touch with and see the nature of no-self, we are always aware of the principle of interdependent co-origination, because interdependent co-origination and no-self are one. All things arise because of their interdependence, and that is why nothing has a separate, independent identity. It is because of our ignorance and hatred that we accuse, reprimand, or slander one another. Each of us is a product of our family, environment, friends, education, culture, and society. These conditions lead to a certain way of seeing things and a certain way of responding to things. When we see this, we have compassion for everyone, including ourselves. We see that if we want someone to change, we also have to help change his or her family, environment, friends, education, culture, and society. We are responsible, directly or indirectly, for each person's consciousness and attitudes. When we see the conditions that have led to that person's consciousness and attitudes, we will know how to help that person. We won't feel angry or blame him. On the contrary, we will try to find ways to help him be free from the constrictions of environment and so forth that have produced his consciousness in that way.

With this kind of insight, we cannot but feel compassion and accept others. How could we continue to see ourselves as the object of false accusations, reprimands, or slander? Even if we are beaten or murdered, when we see deeply and feel compassion like this, we will have a heart of love and will not feel the slightest anger, hatred, or vengeance. If we do not identify ourselves with the Five Aggregates of body, feelings, perceptions, mental formations, and consciousness, others' false accusations, reprimands, or slander will not touch us. The Buddha says, *"If someone were to walk around the grounds of this monastery and pick up the dead branches and dried grass to take home and burn or use in some other way, should we think that it is we ourselves who are being taken home to be burned or used in some way?"*

If criticism, false accusations, and slander are not able to make us angry or vindictive, what about offerings, adoration, praise, and respect? Will they make us proud or arrogant? The answer is still no — not if we are free of the ideas of "I" and "mine."

The Buddha taught, *"If someone respects, honors, or makes offerings to a Tathagata, the Tathagata would not on that account feel pleased. He would think only that someone is doing this because the Tathagata has attained the fruits of awakening and transformation."*

Among the "eight winds" — gain, loss, dishonor, praise, flattery, disgrace, pain, and joy — not one can knock down a person who has realized the teaching of no-self. In the final section of the sutra, the Buddha says, *"The true teachings have been illuminated and made available in the worlds of humans and gods, with nothing lacking. If someone with right understanding penetrates these teachings, the value will be immeasurable. If, at the time of passing from this life, someone has been able to transform the five dull internal formations, in the next life he or she will attain nirvana. That person will arrive at the state of non-returner and will not reenter the cycle of birth and death. If, at the time of passing from this life, someone has been able to transform the three internal forma-*

tions of attachment, aversion, and ignorance, he or she will be born only one more time in the worlds of humans or gods in order to be liberated. If, at the time of passing from this life, someone has been able to attain the fruit of stream-enterer, he or she will not fall again into states of extreme suffering and will surely go in the direction of right awakening. After being born seven times in the worlds of humans or gods, he or she will come to the place of liberation. If, at the time of passing from this life, someone has faith in understanding the teachings, he or she will be born in a blessed world and will continue to progress on the path to highest awakening."

20
CONCLUSION

The *Sutra on Knowing the Better Way to Catch a Snake* is quite important. We are fortunate to have versions of it from two different schools: the Pali version from the Tamrashatiya school and the Chinese version from the Sarvastivada school. By comparing the two, we can discover something close to the original words of the Buddha. It is wonderful to receive these teachings.

In June 1992, I offered a retreat on the theme, "Vipassana in the Mahayana Tradition," in Plum Village, France. We began the retreat with the *Sutra on Knowing the Better Way to Catch a Snake* and found it to be an excellent introduction to Mahayana teachings. The attitude of openness, non-attachment from views, and playfulness offered by this sutra were exactly what we needed as the Dharma door to enter the realm of Mahayana thought and practice. It is so natural to proceed from the *Sutra on Knowing the Better Way to Catch a Snake* to the *Vajracheddika Prajñaparamita Sutra* and to the *Maharatnakuta, Vimalakirti Nirdesha, Avatamsaka,* and *Saddharma Pundarika Sutras.*

Exploring texts like the *Sutra on Knowing the Better Way to Catch a Snake* and the *Sutra on Knowing the Better Way to Live Alone* can help us bring space and fresh air back into the studies and practice of the *Sutta Pitaka* in the Shravaka tradition. As I said in the concluding notes to *Old Path White Clouds,* "Mahayana sutras offer a more liberal and broad way of looking at and understanding the basic teachings of the Buddha. This has the effect of preventing the reification of the teachings, which can come about from a narrow or rigid way of learning and practice. Mahayana sutras help us discover the depths of the *Nikaya* and *Agama* texts. They are like a light projected onto an object under a microscope, an object that has somehow been distorted by artificial means of preservation. Of course the *Nikayas* and *Agamas* are closer to the original form of the Buddha's teachings, but they have been altered and modified by the understanding and practice of the traditions that have passed them down. My wish is that modern scholars and practitioners will be able to restore the true spirit of the Buddha from the available texts of both the Southern and Northern traditions. We need to be open to both traditions."

Parallax Press publishes books on engaged Buddhism and the practice of mindfulness by Thich Nhat Hanh and other authors. As a division of the Unified Buddhist Church, we are committed to making these teachings accessible to everyone and preserving them for future generations. We believe that, in doing so, we help alleviate suffering and create a more peaceful world. For a free catalog, please contact:

Parallax Press
P.O. Box 7355
Berkeley, CA 94707
www.parallax.org
Tel: (800) 863-5290

Monastics and laypeople practice the art of mindful living in the tradition of Thich Nhat Hanh at retreat communities in France and the United States. Individuals, couples, and families are invited to join these communities for a Day of Mindfulness and longer practice periods. For information, please visit www.plumvillage.org or contact:

Plum Village
13 Martineau
33580 Dieulivol, France
info@plumvillage.org

Green Mountain Dharma Center
P.O. Box 182
Hartland Four Corners, VT 05049
mfmaster@vermontel.net
Tel: (802) 436-1103

Deer Park Monastery
2499 Melru Lane
Escondido, CA 92026
deerpark@plumvillage.org
Tel: (760) 291-1003